147 Storytelling Games

and Creative Activities

for the Classroom and the Home

Chris Smith PhD and Kate Barron MEd

www.storytellingschools.com

147 Storytelling Games and Creative Activities for the Classroom and the Home ©
Storytelling Schools Limited 2020

www.storytellingschools.com

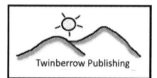

Published by Twinberrow Press
10, Twinberrow Lane, Woodmancote, Gloucestershire,
GL11 4AP
Tel: (+44) 01453 – 544948

Cover and illustrations by Rufus Cooper.

Typesetting and layout by Fiona Gordon.

We have made every effort to trace and deal with any copyright materials. Please let us know if there are any omissions, so that we can make changes to future editions.

We would like to thank Hawthorn Press for their kind permission to use content from The Storytelling School Handbook for Teachers, Smith & Guillain (2014), available as a book and ebook from www.hawthornpress.com.

Acknowledgements

I would like to express gratitude to my own teachers and mentors whose work and approaches helped mould the Storytelling Schools method, in particular the great storyteller Ben Haggerty, the wonderful storytelling-in-therapy expert Alida Gersie and the brilliant storytelling educator Pie Corbett. Thanks also to Storytelling Schools trainers – Adam Guillain, Jules Pottle, Nanette Noonan and co-author Kate Barron - who have all made huge contributions to the development of the method.

All of the activities in this booklet have been tried and tested and evolved over many years; accordingly, we have not tried to reference each with an arbitrary original source.

Last but not least, thank you to the hundreds of head teachers, thousands of teachers and tens of thousands of students around the UK and beyond who have embraced this method of learning. Also, thanks to the parents and home educators who have brought this approach into their homes. May the crucial skills of oracy, creativity and literacy flourish, allowing students to enjoy their learning and better fulfil their present and future potential.

Chris Smith PhD
Director
Storytelling Schools Limited
UK

Storytelling Schools ™ is an educational method where oral storytelling is placed at the heart of learning. Our model integrates elements from the creative arts and educational sciences into a whole school method in a lively, dynamic and inclusive way. Educators using our method report huge gains in both academic and personal development. In this approach, oracy and creativity provide the springboards for learning both language and subject content across the curriculum. We provide resources, support and training to organisations and individuals wishing to adopt the method.

**For more information visit
www.storytellingschools.com**

Contents

Introduction   1

Speaking and Listening Games   6

Re-telling a Story by Heart   10

Story Comprehension   16

Drama   22

Music   26

Movement   29

Poetry   32

Art, Design and Digital   37

Other Curriculum Links   40

Story Writing   43

Story Recycling   49

Story Creation   52

References   58

Glossary   59

Annex 1. Plot Matrix Planning Sheet   62

Annex 2. The Seven Basic Plots Planning Grids   63

Annex 3. Detailed Index   64

Annex 4. Alphabetical Index   69

Introduction

Storytelling games and creative activities are an invaluable part of every educator's toolkit. They can be an engaging hook to launch a subject, getting students involved in learning the language and concepts of a topic. They can be used to deepen knowledge and understanding of a subject and to practise applying that knowledge in new creative contexts. They can also be used as springboards for various writing activities: by practising a piece verbally before writing, there is a chance for the story to evolve and take form before putting pen to paper. Consequently, by the time students start writing they can focus on transcription without having to worry about content or structure.

For parents too, these activities provide an opportunity to connect, communicate and create within the family. They offer ways to enable a rich spoken language environment within the home: one of the key determinants of educational and professional success. They also provide a repertoire of playful ways of being together, whether on walks, car journeys, at bedtime or around the kitchen table on rainy days. Storytelling and storymaking with your children are precious and memorable gifts for your family.

Whether you are teaching early years, primary or secondary students or involved in home study, adding such games and activities to your repertoire will make your sessions more lively, engaging and creative. In addition, workshop leaders may use them as ice breakers, energisers or warm ups. They also provide formats for creative team building exercises.

The games and activities within this collection have all been tried and tested within the Storytelling Schools™ programme in the UK. When schools adopt the Storytelling Schools method, they normally embrace many of these activities as part of their normal teaching routine.

The aim of this book is to offer these activities to the wider audience of educators who would like to pick and mix these activities in any way they choose to suit their own purposes.

We have organised the book into the following sections, with a detailed index at the back for easy reference. In practice there is plenty of overlap in categories, as speaking activities are often linked to drama and writing.

- Speaking and listening games
- Re-telling a story by heart
- Story comprehension
- Drama
- Music
- Movement
- Poetry
- Art, design and digital
- Other curriculum links
- Story writing
- Story recycling
- Story creation

Most of the activities here can be completed in 40 minutes or less, although sometimes we suggest links to further writing which might take a little longer. Descriptions are short and to the point, just giving an outline of the idea for educators to flesh out and adapt as they see fit.

May you enjoy using these games to better engage and inspire your students. They are all there to ignite that creative spark which brings playfulness, pleasure and creativity to learning.

Some readers may be interested in knowing something about the Storytelling Schools method. In summary, the approach works like this:

- First, students learn to **TELL** the story from memory, improvising their own fluent way of telling rather than rote learning. In this way, students master the language and concepts within a story.

- Then comes the **DEEPENING** stage, where students practise applying the language and ideas of the story through various creative activities. These might include some of the drama, art, design, poetry, music and movement activities listed in this collection.

- After that, students may plan and **WRITE** their own versions of the story, channelling the rich bank of language and ideas they have learned into their text.

- Alternatively, students may **RECYCLE** the story, keeping the pattern but changing some or all of the content, for example changing 'Little Red Riding Hood and the Wolf' into 'Little Red Astronaut and the Alien'.

- Finally, students may be asked to **CREATE** a brand new story, not based on an existing story but, rather, made up fresh. Often, things which have been learned in the earlier stages can be independently applied here.

Fig. 1 below shows this teaching model and the typical sequence of activities.

Fig. 1 - Teaching Model

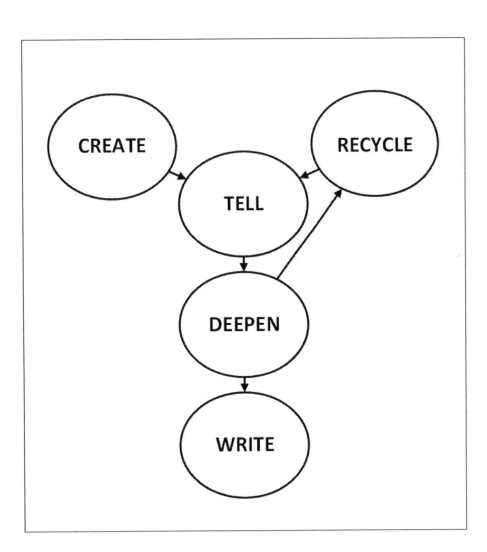

Notes for Parents and Home Educators

The instructions for these activities are mostly given for the classroom teacher working with groups of about 30 or so students. Often in a classroom situation, the activities are explained and demonstrated to everyone, then groups or pairs try them out before reporting back to the whole class.

As a parent or home educator, you'll need to adapt these instructions for your situation. For example, if you are working with just one or two children you might simply explain about the activity and then practise it together with the children; no need for small groups and the 'report back' stage. The purpose of your role is to encourage the children to become actively involved in the exercise. First, demonstrate the activity so they can see how you do it and learn from your example. After that encourage them to have a go themselves, allowing them – step by step – to master the skills involved.

One of the satisfying things about activities like these can be for children to show their creative output to an audience, receiving appreciation and support as a result. In the home situation this might be another family member or friend who joins the group for this when needed. Other options could be to record the performance digitally so that it can be shared or shown to others later. Please don't be put off by the references to teachers and students; adapt and adjust the activities to suit your situation.

Speaking and Listening Games

Speaking and Listening Games

These games can be used as warm up activities, getting the speaking and listening going in pairs and groups before starting the main activity. In this way, they can also be used to practise and develop the listening skills which are crucial to the future development of your students, while building confidence in fluent speech. They are also a good way to get used to working collaboratively: a really important skill for everyone to learn.

Tell me more

Work in pairs. The first person speaks a sentence about themselves. The listener chooses a word from the sentence and says, 'Tell me more about ....' adding the chosen word. The first person speaks another sentence about the new word and again the listener chooses a word and says, 'Tell me more about ...' choosing a word from the sentence they have just heard. If the pair gets stuck then start again. After a while swap roles.

For example, an exchange might go:

A. I live in London.
B. Tell me more (TMM) about London.
A. London is a big noisy city.
B. TMM about noisy.
A. The cars and buses make loud noises and bad smells all day. I hate it.
B. TMM about hate.

And so on...

Consider writing a simple *tell-me-more* poem using a word from each line to start the next. For example:

I live in London.
London is so vast and noisy.
Noisy cars crowd the streets.
Streets are packed with people, always in a hurry.
Hurry here, hurry there, never getting anywhere.

Tell me more lies

Repeat 'Tell me more', but this time the first person creates a new name and character for themselves and starts with, "My name is ... and I like ....". Then the game continues as before with the first person making things up about their character or anything else that comes up.

For example:

A. My name is Billy and I like dancing.
B. TMM about dancing.
A. I like to dance on my roof when the moon is full.
B. TMM about moon.
A. When the moon is full a dragon flies down from the mountains to dance with me.
B. TMM about dragon.

And so on ...

Again, consider writing a *tell-me-more* poem about an imagined character using the same principle.

Tell me more fiction

Repeat 'tell me more' for a known fictional character. See if you can stick to what is known about the character, or else make it up.

Fortunately - unfortunately

Sit in a small circle. The first person starts off with a character and an unfortunate event. The next one has something fortunate happen; the next adds something unfortunate and so on. Do not kill the character. At the end retell some of the stories to the whole class and ask listeners to choose their favourite bits.

Why - because

Work in pairs. The first person says a sentence and the partner asks why. The first person answers the question using 'because' and the partner asks why again. Keep going for a while. Then, pair up with a second pair explaining all the causes using 'why / because' and perhaps try using other causal connectives. This task could then be linked to explanatory writing.

Why - because for fiction

Choose a sentence about a story you know and repeat the 'why / because' process. See how far you can get. Consider linking to an explanation piece.

City of Rome

Sit in a circle of 4-10 people. Close your eyes.

The first person says, 'In the City of Rome there is a ...' and finishes the sentence describing something visual for example, 'a man holding an umbrella'.

The next person describes the previous picture and adds something like this:

'In the City of Rome there is a man is holding an umbrella. An eagle hovers above him'.

Keep going like this, describing the existing picture and adding something. **Important: it is not about word for word memory, it's more about visualising the picture**. You can zoom in on detail or zoom out to the landscape. See how long you can continue. Remember to keep the picture static or it can get muddled.

Afterwards, consider drawing or painting the scene, or using it as a starting point for making up a story.

Spot the lie

Tell a true story about yourself and sneak in three lies. Can your partner guess the lies?

Repetition

Tell a story without repeating a noun or adjective. The listener stops you when they spot one and it's their turn. How far can you get? Find out with a timer.

Re-telling a Story by Heart

Re-telling a Story by Heart

These exercises offer different ways to teach students how to tell a story from memory once it has been heard. It achieves the learning of language, structure and content in a single activity. As a teacher, don't forget to demonstrate the storytelling yourself so that students can learn from watching you.

Tell it and map it

Tell the class a story, and then demonstrate creating a simple story map together. Have volunteers practise retelling from the map with feedback on the listener's favourite bits. Then, let everyone independently make their own map, tell from their map in pairs, and give feedback on their favourite bits. Take a maximum of five minutes for the mapping.

Fig. 2 shows an example of a story map. Notice how the pictures are simple and quick.

Fig. 2 Story Map for The Three Little Pigs

Tell it and step it

Tell the class a story or remind them of a story from a map if it is already known. Show them how to step a story with phrases (i.e. make a gesture and a phrase for the first scene, then step forward and make a gesture and a phrase to represent the second scene and so on). Have students practise in twos or threes then perform back to the class with appreciation of favourite movements or phrases. Repeat for stepping with a sound effect for each step. Finally, step silently just doing the actions.

Fig. 3 Example of Stepping Using Little Red Riding Hood.

Tell it in pairs with a talking stick

Take a known story which has been mapped and stepped. Show them how to tell with a talking stick in pairs, passing the story along by passing the stick back and forth. Each student speaks a few sentences, embellishing the story if they like, and then passes the story back to their partner. Only the stick holder may speak! Practise in pairs, then have pairs perform to the class or to other pairs for appreciative feedback about favourite moments.

Tell it in a talking circle

Take a known story which has been mapped and stepped. Show students how to tell with a talking stick, passing the story on every few sentences and embellishing the story in new ways. Divide the class into groups and have each group retell the story by themselves in their talking circle. Afterwards, discuss favourite moments and phrases.

Story circle performance

Get four people to perform a known story to the class with a talking stick. Get feedback on favourite phrases and gestures afterwards. Don't worry if they miss a bit. Repeat once or twice.

Tell another class a story

Visit another class and have your students tell them a story. Either have pairs telling another pair or individuals telling to a small group of listeners, depending on confidence. Always ask for positive feedback about favourite things afterwards.

Card sorting

Make a set of cards with pictures from a story map. Distribute and get the students to sort the cards and retell the story from them.

Learn from a storyteller clip

Listen to a clip of a storyteller telling a story. Let the students analyse what the storyteller is doing, then apply those lessons to telling their own story.

Reflecting circle retelling

Stand in a circle and the teacher tells a story, one sentence at a time, with a gesture for each sentence. The group repeats each gesture and sentence like an echo. Repeat with different tasks like: re-tell in the first person, speech only or description only. Let students have a go at leading the telling. Here's an example of a series of gestures to retell The Three Little Pigs.

Fig. 4 Gestures for Retelling The Three Little Pigs

Story Sentences	Gestures
Once upon a **time**, there were **three** little **pigs**.	**Time**-point to wrist. **Three**- 3 fingers. **Pigs**- touch nose.
Mama said, "Go build a **house**.	**Mama** – show skirt with hands. **House** – arms make roof above head.
Build it **strong**, there's **danger** in the world."	**Strong** – bend the arm showing off bicep muscle.
The **first** little **pig** built a **house** out of **straw**.	**First** – one finger. **Straw** – mime touching a piece of straw.
Along came the **wolf** and **ate** him up. "**Yum-yum,** that tasted good."	**Wolf**- mime claws and roaring. **Ate**- mime eating. **Yum-yum** - rub tummy.
The **second** little **pig** built a **house** out of **twigs**.	**Second** – two fingers. **Twigs** – mime touching a thicker piece of wood.
Along came the **wolf** and **ate** him up. "**Yum yum,** that tasted good."	**Wolf**- mime claws and roaring. **Ate**- mime eating. **Yum-yum** - rub tummy.
The **third** little **pig** built a house out of **bricks**.	**Third**- 3 fingers. **Bricks**- mime the shape of a brick with hands.

Along came the **wolf** and **couldn't eat** him up.	**Couldn't** – mime a wagging finger meaning 'no'.
The **pig** was **happy** and safe.	**Happy** – smile with fingers showing smile.
And the **wolf went home.**	**Went home** – wave goodbye.

N.B. You can also use this format to retell the outline of a more complex story. It doesn't always have to be word for word retelling of the whole thing. Just use key moments.

Story Comprehension

Story Comprehension

Once a story is known by the class, these activities provide ways to explore how the story works, teaching the students to develop their 'thinking like a writer' skills, which will help them when they plan their own stories.

Reflecting circle for story appreciation

Have the students stand in a circle to share their favourite moments from a story in a reflecting circle. The first student makes a gesture and phrase or sound which evokes their favourite moment and the rest of the circle makes the same gesture or sound back to them. Continue around the circle until everyone has had a go.

Mood map

Create a mood map of a story and plot the moods on a graph with happy up and sad down. Discuss. Repeat for the moods of different characters, charting how the emotions of each change through the story. Fig. 5 shows an example.

Fig. 5 Mood Map for Little Red Riding Hood

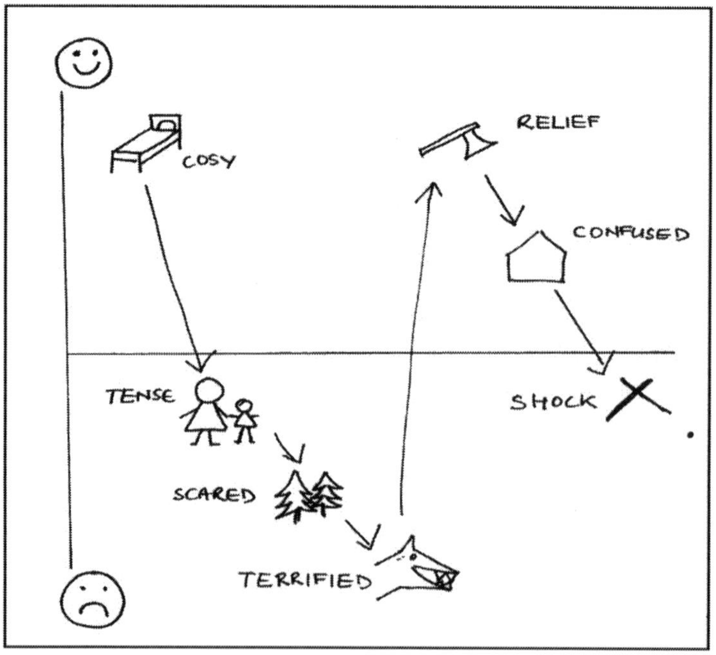

Plot matrix

Choose a story which the class knows and have them analyse how the story works using the Plot Matrix. This is a nine box grid which summaries the main elements which make many stories work, shown below. You might use prompts like this to evoke suggestions from the class:

- Is the setting clear?
- Is the (inner) character quality clear and suitable?
- Is the problem important enough?
- Do the setbacks stretch out the drama?
- Is the helper involved?
- Does the solution satisfy?
- Are the consequences of the solution clear in the ending?
- Is the learning thread clear?

Fig. 6 The Plot Matrix

Where?	Who?	What's the problem?
Setback 1	Setback 2	Helpers
Solution	Ending	Learning

You can fill these boxes in with either words or pictures. Fig. 7 shows an example of each.

Fig. 7 Plot Matrix for Little Red Riding hood

↑↑	foolish	
	⌂	
RIP		

Forest	Foolish girl	Death by wolf
First meeting	In the cottage	woodcutter
Death	Sadness	Think and look!

Character by role on the wall

Use a large piece of paper to draw around a student (the outline represents a character from a story). Inside the outline brainstorm and write words to describe the personality/feelings of the character. On the outside, brainstorm and write words that describe physical appearance. Pin on the wall for all to see. Repeat for all characters. Use as a guide for character writing. This can also be done on a smaller piece of paper as an individual or small group exercise.

Character by phone

Role play being a character in the story describing a second character to a friend on the phone. The job of the friend is to ask questions about the second character to build up a picture of what it looks like, smells like, sounds like, feels like, how it behaves and what is it like.

For example, let's say Little Red Riding Hood has just seen the wolf and calls a friend. The dialogue might go like this:

A. Hi, it's me Red Riding Hood.
B. Hi there. What are you up to?
A. I just saw a wolf in the wood.
B. Gosh, what did it look like?
A. It was huge, taller than me with red staring eyes and long sharp claws.
B. What was it doing?
A. It stood there, growling at me.

And so on…

After the demonstration, let the students have a go in pairs, then replay a few to the class.

Character profile

Role play being a reporter explaining about what a particular character is like. Have pairs practise and playback to the class. Chart up favourite phrases. Then have everyone write a newspaper feature about the qualities of the character.

Quiz

Invent a quiz about a story you are studying and give it to the class.

Character from movie clip

Show a clip of a character doing something that shows what kind of person they are: i.e. what is their 'quality'? Students then write a character profile. Share them in groups and give feedback on how the profile shows the character quality.

Ending debate

Choose three endings for a story and have the class debate which is best and why. Explore what makes an ending satisfying.

Tweet re-telling

Have students summarise a story in a series of 5 -10 tweets (i.e. maximum 280 characters)

Movie plot summary

Take a movie the class knows, map the plot out and retell it from the map, then write a plot summary.

Basic plots

The "basic plots" is a term coined by Booker (2004) to suggest seven common plot types. They are:

- Voyage and return
- Rags to riches
- Overcoming the monster
- Comedy
- Tragedy
- Quest
- Rebirth

See Annex 2 for more details of the types.

Choose a story the students know and discuss which of the basic plot types fits the story best.

Drama

Drama

Drama is a tried and tested way of retelling and exploring a story in a varied and engaging way. It allows students to take the language, imagination and understanding they have learned about a story and apply it in a wide variety of ways. Here are a few popular exercises.

Whole class re-enactment

Have the class sit or stand in a circle. You tell a story and choose students to mime or enact the various characters, events or objects in the story as you name them. E.g., include trees, oceans, animals, buildings as well as the main action. Start off with mime, then let the characters begin to speak. Discuss favourite moments at the end.

Re-enactment and word-storming

Perform a whole class re-enactment and, every now and then, stop the action and ask the class to brainstorm words and phrases to describe what is happening. For example, you might ask what the character is feeling; what the character is thinking; what the character is seeing or hearing and so on. You might chart up the ideas for future reference.

Phone home

Role play a character calling home and telling a parent what happened to them, how they felt and what they thought. The parents' job is to evoke, in sequence, what happened and the character's thoughts/feelings at the time. Let students practise in pairs, then play back to the class with appreciation of favourite phrases.

Dialogue role play

Role play improvising the dialogue at a particular moment in a story. Show the class how to extend and expand the dialogue as a way of showing character and mood. Then, let them practise in pairs and play back to the class for appreciation. Afterwards, you might ask students to have a go at writing the dialogue.

Hot seat

Demonstrate hot-seating a character with a clear purpose and focus (the teacher is in role as a character and the students ask questions). Initially, there can be a focus on finding out three things at the various points in the story:

- what the character did,
- how the character felt, and
- what the character thought.

Later, hot-seating can be used to explore intention or learning. The main thing is to be clear about the purpose of the hot-seating.

Once the teacher has demonstrated being in the hot seat, let students have a go.

Job interview

Role play a character applying for a job, maybe at your school. Then, divide the class into groups and let everyone have a go. Perhaps play back a few to the whole class. You might then give them a writing task where they write a letter as that character, applying for a job of their choice.

Puppet retelling

Have each group make simple puppets for each character in a story using paper, colours, sticky tape and ice cream sticks. Re-enact the story using the puppets and review.

Freeze-frames

Divide up a story into key moments, divide the class into groups and allocate one moment to each group. Demonstrate how to create a freeze-frame, get each group to create one for their moment and then perform back the whole story, frame by frame.

You might then repeat and have the class brainstorm words for each moment and chart them up for future writing.

Acting out key scenes

Divide up a story into scenes, divide the class into groups and allocate one scene to each group. Have each group rehearse and perform their scene with action and dialogue. List favourite phrases and chart them up.

TV chat show improvisation

Role play a TV chat show involving characters from your story. If students don't know any chat shows, then show them a clip of one. Explore how the characters would react to different situations based on their character quality.

This is Your Life

Pick a character from a story and then role play how a 'This is Your Life' TV show retells the character's life story. Then, have the students practise in groups and perform back to the class.

Courtroom drama

Choose a story where someone is at fault. Demonstrate role-playing being the lawyer. Plan and present a summary of the case for the defence to the court, then let your students have a go. Repeat for the prosecution.

Mannequin modelling

In a group, the 'director' moves the body shape of the students by hand until they are in the shape of a story scene. Then take a photo. Start off demonstrating being the director then let groups create their own shows. Let each group make a slide show and add narration.

Toys and props

Get some simple toys and props and demonstrate retelling a story in freeze-frames, photographing each frame. Let groups have a go, maybe creating a slide show and adding narration.

Tell and mime

Demonstrate one person telling a story while a partner or a group mimes it. Divide into groups for practice and play back.

Music

Music

Music provides a lovely way to breathe life into a story. These three exercises require no musical training and offer the chance for students to experience the fun of making up songs and sounds around a story.

Fitting songs to the steps

Step through a story with a word and gesture for each step (see p.11), and then get the class or groups to think of songs they know that will fit with each step. For example, if there is a step with a monster they might sing 'Thriller' or 'Monster Mash'. If there is a step with a battle they might sing 'Waterloo'. Perform a song for each step, with actions, to appreciative feedback.

Creating songs to the steps

Step or map a story, then choose a simple song everyone knows. Assign a group to each step and get them to make up words for that scene that fit with the song. There is no need to rhyme the lines.

For example, retelling Little Red Riding hood to the tune of Twinkle, Twinkle, Little Star, a verse could be:

"Little Red Riding Hood,

Feeling frightened in the wood.

What is that, up ahead?

Could it be a scary wolf?

Little Red Riding Hood,

Feeling frightened in the wood"

Sing the verses in sequence and appreciate.

Instruments and soundscapes

Step or map a story and then assign a step to each group. Using whatever instruments you have, let each group create a sound or music piece for their step. Perform the story using the instrumental pieces as links between the re-telling of each section.

Repeat using the music as a basis for miming the story with each group miming their own section.

Movement

Movement

For some students, physicality and movement are important ways to get involved with a story. Students who are reluctant readers and writers may love to move and dance. These simple exercises offer ways to get movement and dance happening in your classroom.

Reflecting circle

Stand in a circle. The teacher makes a series of simple, clear gestures which retell a story. After each gesture the class copies like an echo. Then let students lead with their own gestures.

Story Stepping

Step through a story making a clear gesture to represent each scene with each step (see p.11 for example). Let students make up their own steps.

Class dance

Choose a series of gestures and map them for the class with simple stick figures. Now, practise a simple dance step, say one step to the side and one step back, and then make the gestures while doing the dance step. Finally, when ready, put on a suitable piece of music and have the whole class dance in unison.

Discuss the experience and ways to improve the dance.

Group dance

Repeat the class dance exercise in small groups so that every group creates their own individual dance piece. Let groups perform back to the class to appreciative feedback about favourite movements.

Steps into Dance

Take the gestures from the story stepping (see p.11) and turn them into a dance by adding some rhythmic dance steps and finding a suitable dance track.

Song into dance

Let's say the class has made up a song to retell a whole story. Divide into groups and give each group a verse. Get each group to make clear gestures to go with their verse so they can sing it and move to it at the same time. Then ask each group to just make the gestures while the whole class hums the tune (no words). Repeat till the class can dance the whole story together.

After that, choose a new piece of music and have the class dance to it with the same gestures. Remember, get them to move their feet a little to make it into a dance.

Group dance (by genre)

Repeat the group dance but show the class some videos of dance routines: for example, pop, jazz, urban or simple hip-hop routines - and then look at adapting the moves to a story. Each group creates their own version.

.

Poetry

Poetry

Poetry is a great way to practise playing with words, teaching precision, concision and how to create a strong impact on the reader. Using a story as a context, there is no limit to the ways that poetry can be used to re-tell and explore. The following are some of the poetic forms you might consider for these exercises. They are all relatively simple and quick to use. Don't worry about rhyming until the students are ready.

- Word pattern poems are defined by the number of words in each line and the number of lines. For example, a 3-4-3-4 poem might be:

   Poor little girl
   Lost in the wood
   Something up ahead
   Heart begins to quicken

- The modern cinquain is a particular version of the word pattern poem with a 1-2-3-4-1 pattern where line one is the title, line 2 is about the title, line 3 is an action and line 4 is a feeling. Finally line 5 recalls the title again. For example:

   Granny
   Waiting, knitting
   Door creaks open
   Heart beats like a drum
   Granny

- List poems are easy and flexible and simply consist of lists around a theme of a place or a character. For example, using the wolf:

   He is always hungry
   His teeth are like razors
   His eyes are cold and dark
   His claws are sharp like knives
   His heart cares nothing for human life

- Haikus are simple three-line poems with a 5-7-5 syllable pattern. For example:

    > I stare at his eyes
    > Breath stops and body freezes
    > No escape for me

- Kennings use a hyphenated descriptive couplet at the start of each line, often to describe a character. For example, for the wolf it might be:

    > Dark-hunter
    > Death-maker
    > Heart-breaker
    > Breath-taker

    > Or

    > Dark-hunter, looking in the shadows
    > Death-maker, relentlessly killing
    > Heart-breaker, drawing grief in his wake
    > Breath-taker, feasting on someone's children

- ABC poems use a letter sequence to start of each line. For example:

    > A girl is walking.
    > Behind her something stirs.
    > Could it be a squirrel or a bird?
    > Don't think about it!
    > Everything will be alright!

    > You can use this form to spell out names or words and write about them (acrostic poems).

- With free verse you can do what you like, but you might like to give example for your students to emulate or you may just get prose!

Word pattern poem

Decide on a word pattern poem based on a number of lines and words, for example, four lines with a 3-4-3-4 words, respectively. Divide up a story and assign each to a group. The job of each group is to create a 3-4-3-4 poem about that moment in the story. You might ask for specific things (action, feeling, multisensory descriptions) or leave the choice open.

Perform the poems in sequence to create a narrative poem. Maybe write up the whole poem and edit as a class.

Poem into song

Have each group create a word pattern poem so that the whole of a story is retold, then choose a suitable tune and have them revise the poem so it fits with the rhythm of the song. Sing through the story as a whole class.

Recycle a poem

Show the class a suitable poem and review it's form together. Then, show how to use the pattern to make up a poem about a story moment. Let everyone make up their own.

Poem from picture

Show a picture of a story moment and create a simple poem about it with the class. Let everyone create their own version. Share and review. Start with simple formats like list poems; no need to make the lines rhyme.

Narrative poem from pictures

Make or find a series of story pictures which retell a story from start to finish and distribute one picture to each group. Each group then creates a poem about that moment. String them all together into a single poem to retell the whole story.

Movie poem

Take a movie and summarise it with the plot matrix (p.17), then retell it in nine sentences. Turn the sentences into a poem.

Book poem

Take a literature story and summarise it with the plot matrix, then retell it in 9 sentences. Make a nine line list poem.

Poem from a name (acrostic)

Choose a character from a story and use their name to create an 'ABC' poem describing things about the character. For example:

> **W**ild and dangerous
> **O**ur most feared foe
> **L**ooking for prey
> **F**angs at the ready.

Question poem

Use a story map to create a story-poem, using only questions.

Praise poem

Make up praise poems to the various characters in a story.

Bragging poems

Make up bragging/boasting poems for the characters.

Art, Design and Digital

Art, Design and Digital

Creating sketches, pictures, paintings and models of a story gives students a chance to vividly re-imagine the story elements while giving context and meaning to their creations. Increasingly, the digital world provides a huge range of options for such creative expression.

Story picture exhibition

Divide up a story into moments or scenes. Groups are allocated one scene each and create pictures, poems, models, songs and dances about that scene. Make an exhibition and invite other classes and parents to be guided through, with a guide telling the story. Use talking buttons and tablets to capture sound and vision as needed.

Cartoon re-telling

Using a story map as the basis, have each student create a cartoon retelling the story with speech bubbles and emojis.

Giant story map

Create a giant story map on the wall with groups painting or collaging different scenes of the story.

Shoe box setting

Have groups make peep hole shoe box settings for various story moments. Invite visitors and have students tell them the story as they peep from box to box.

Prop making

Have the class make props to use when retelling a story.

Stop-start

Retell stories using stop-start animation with people, puppets or models.

Lego or plasticine re-telling

Have the class make a story exhibition from plasticine or Lego, creating a model for each scene. Add labels and invite visitors.

Green screen

Students make videos telling a story in front of a green screen and then splice in backdrops to go with the story from the internet.

Record storytelling

Record videos of students telling a story, then put in a digital file for each student. Look back every year and discuss progress.

Other Curriculum Links

Other Curriculum Links

There is no limit to how far a story can be used as a context for teaching across the curriculum. Here are some popular angles to try, using the pleasure and knowledge of the story as a springboard for interest, engagement and wider learnings.

Research

Choose subjects related to a story and ask students to research it online, then create a verbal or written presentation about what they learned.

Reading

Provide a set of readings related to the content of a story. Have students read and present their findings verbally or in writing.

Non-fiction

Ask students to create discussions, persuasions, instructions, explanations, recounts or information reports about something in a story. Make an oral or written presentation.

Experiences

Expose the class to the direct experience of something related to a story. This might be a place (woodland), an object (axe, wolf skin), or perhaps video clips of things related to the story. Brainstorm descriptive words after the experience and consider linking to a writing task.

Science

Choose an element of a story that can link to part of the science curriculum (biology, chemistry, physics). Teach that science using the story as a starting point.

Values

Choose a value illustrated by a story and discuss it with the class. Use this as a springboard for oral or written presentations about the value.

History

Choose something in a story for which a historical perspective can be taught (wolves, woods, childhood). Teach the class this historical dimension with the story as the springboard.

Geography

Choose an element of a story that can link to part of the geography curriculum. Teach the geography using the story as a starting point. For example, deserts, oceans or cities.

Maths

Choose something maths-related in a story that you want to teach. Find a way to teach it using the story as a springboard (for example, distance, journey time and speed problems).

Citizenship

Is there something in a story that can illustrate one aspect of citizenship (rule of law, right to protection)? Think of a way to teach it using the story as the springboard.

Other languages

Retell a story at a suitable level in a different language.

Emotional literacy

Talk about and map the emotions of the characters in a story (see mood map p.16). Discuss what we can learn from the story about feelings and their expression. Have the students discuss what they would do differently.

Story Writing

Story Writing

Once a student has got to know a story, there is no limit to the range of writing tasks that can be used to retell and re-explore the tale. Here are a few popular exercises which can also be used for recycled and created stories.

Mood mapping and writing

Create a mood map of a story (see p.16) and practise writing short pieces for each mood using multisensory descriptions, show-don't-tell, as well as the thoughts and feelings of the characters and narrator. Share and review.

Multisensory writing

Choose a moment in a story and brainstorm language for the various senses at that moment (see, hear, smell, taste, touch). Chart the words up on a grid. Then create a piece of multi-sensory writing using the words as a resource. Next, divide up the story into groups and have each group repeat for their section. Share and review.

Wanted poster

With the class, create a 'WANTED!' poster for a particular character with a clear visual description using some pictures and phrases. Then let everyone create their own.

Postcards home

Have each student design and write postcards that might be sent home by characters at a given moment in a story. The picture is of the place and the text is about what happened. Share and explore.

Diary entry

Have each student write a short diary entry in role as the character at a given moment in a story. Explore thoughts and feelings and share with the class.

Monologue

Write a short monologue in role as character at a particular story moment. Rehearse orally first.

Thought and speech bubbles

Have each student write thoughts and feelings speech bubbles for characters at particular moments in a story. Rehearse orally first.

Setting

Demonstrate writing about various settings in a story using multi-sensory descriptions. Have students practise their own and share with the class.

Text messaging

Create a dialogue from a story using text messaging.

Descriptive zooming

Choose a story moment and draw a picture of it. Next, zoom in to one part of the picture and draw a new one adding more details. Then, zoom out and draw a third picture to show what might be around the first picture. Now, create a piece of writing which zooms in and out. Have each student try for a particular moment in the story. Discuss the effect on the writing.

Story pitch

Get students to create a digital or written advert pitching a story in order to persuade someone to read it.

Movie pitch

How would you make a story into a movie? Role play pitching the idea orally to a Hollywood company and then write the pitch. Have groups practise the role play, and then write their own pitch.

Facebook / Instagram

Have students retell a story using Facebook or Instagram posts.

Newspaper report

Demonstrate creating newspaper reports about a story or an element of it. It could be a recount of what happened, a general report about it or a persuasion editorial piece on opinion. First show the genre, then demonstrate the writing before letting the students have a go.

Play script

Get students to write a script for a section of a story as if it were going to be performed as a play or film.

Texts

Get students to create a set of texts to and from a friend to retell a story.

Emails

Have students create a set of short emails to and from a friend to retell a story.

Newspaper article

Show the class a newspaper article. Explore the structure and language used. Then the students can create their own newspaper article about something in a story.

Rewrite a song-story

Choose a song-story that the class loves. Listen to a song-story once or twice then map, step and tell it as prose. Then have each student write up the prose version.

Flashback writing

Give the class a beginning which contains the ending of a story. Have them write the rest of the story as flashbacks or in a backwards time sequence.

Mood practice

Choose a particular section of a story which the class knows and have them rewrite it in order to evoke a new mood. For example, re-write Little Red Riding Hood meeting the wolf but the interaction is with courage instead of fear.

Setting writing

Choose a place you know and write an opening paragraph describing it as the setting for a story.

Suspense writing practice

Write a piece of suspense using hints, unanswered questions and events that cannot be explained.

Dilemma writing

Choose a story where there is a difficult choice and generate ideas for what the character is thinking about the different choices. String them together into a thought piece or soliloquy.

Multisensory openings

Write a story opening using *all* 5 senses.

Mono-sensory openings

Write an opening using only *one* of the 5 senses.

Dialogue between first and last

Give the first and last line of a dialogue and have the group write the rest of the dialogue.

Show-don't-tell mood practice

Read a 'show-don't-tell' piece to the class which evokes a particular mood. Let the students guess the mood. Give each student a mood to evoke themselves in writing, then let the class guess the mood when they read it out.

Show-don't-tell character practice

Shared write a 'show-don't-tell' piece to evoke a character quality (e.g. brave, smart, nervous) with actions, thoughts and feelings. Then, distribute various character qualities and let students create their own written piece. Read them to the class and then let the class guess the quality.

Dating site profile

Demonstrate writing a profile of the character for a dating site. Get the students to have a go for one of the characters in a story.

Obituary

Get students to write an obituary for a character from a story.

Object writing

Find an object from a story and create a multi-sensory word list about it with the class. Have each student create a short piece of writing about the object.

Therapist advice

Choose a problem that a character has and demonstrate writing an advice letter from their therapist about it. Then distribute a range of problems and let each student write an advice letter to the character.

·

Story Recycling

Story Recycling

Story recycling means taking an existing story and making a new one out of it, so that the student learns to keep the structure and change the content: a way of moving towards fluent story making. There are various popular ways to do this:

- **Simple substitution** means changing one thing in the story but leaving everything else the same (i.e. the wolf becomes a human predator or the girl becomes a boy).
- **Complex substitution** means that you change one thing in the story, but then you have to change other things too for the story to work. This helps students learn about story cohesion. For example, if the wolf becomes a small bird then everything else has to change for the story to work. For example, the girl might become the Little Red Caterpillar.
- **Plot recycling** means taking the overall pattern of the story and making up a new story to fit the pattern. For example, let's say the Red Riding Hood pattern is a journey and two encounters with danger: we might turn it into Little Red Mermaid and the Big Bad Shark.
- **Point of view** means retelling the story from a character's point of view, usually in the first person.
- **Prequel and sequel writing** means thinking about what might have happened before or after the story.

Here are some popular exercises.

Reset in a modern context

Reset a fairy tale or classic story in a modern context, recycling the pattern and changing the contents.

Find a new ending

Tell the class half a story and have them invent new endings. Share and review.

Recycle with substitution

Plot out a story on a plot matrix (p. 17). Change one thing and see how it changes the whole story. Alternatively, do the same thing using a story map.

Recycle with plot pattern

Use plot recycling to create a new story from an old one. First, decide on the plot pattern of your story. For example, the pattern of The Three Little Pigs and the Big Bad Wolf might be *a story about three brothers all following instructions to do something to keep safe*. Now think of ways to create a new story using that original pattern. For example, the new story could be *The Three Little Astronauts and The Big Bad Alien and how they built their space rockets*.

Recycle with a new point of view

Retell a story from one character's point of view.

Back-stories

Choose a character from a story and invent their back-story. Demonstrate making one up with the class then have the students write their own and share with the class. Discuss.

Story Creation

Story Creation

With story creation, students make up fresh stories with complete freedom. Here the Plot Matrix can be used as a guide to help students plan their stories. Key prompts for each section are suggested below:

Where?	Who?	What problem?
What is the place like where the story happens?	Who is the main character and what is their inner quality?	What important problem does the character face? Why does it matter?
Setback 1	**Setback 2**	**Helper**
How does the middle of the story build the drama with setbacks and difficulties?	How does the middle of the story build the drama with setbacks and difficulties?	Is there a character, object or quality which helps the character solve the problem?
Solution	**Ending**	**Learning**
How can the problem be solved in a satisfying way (or not)?	What are the consequences of the solution or non-solution?	Is there a learning thread which runs through the story?

You can print off blank plot matrix planning sheets from Annex 1.

Story from character and object

Choose a character and an object and demonstrate making up a story using the plot matrix. Let the students have a go themselves and tell back to class.

Shared story-making from an object

Choose an object and make up a story by asking the group questions including plot matrix questions. Let the students have a go.

Word story circle

Sit in a circle or 4-10 people. One starts with a word and the next in the circle adds a word. In this way, create a story. Remember to add full stops every now and then. Don't kill the main character. At the end, discuss what worked and why.

Sentence story circle

Sit in a circle of 4-10 people. One starts with a sentence introducing a character and the next in the circle adds the next sentence. In this way, create a story. Don't kill the main character. At the end discuss what worked and why.

Fortunately - unfortunately

Sit in a small circle. The first person starts off with a character and an unfortunate event. The next one has something fortunate happen. The next adds something unfortunate and so on. Don't kill the character. At the end retell the whole thing and choose favourite bits.

Story from known object

Choose an object from a known story and create a new story together as a class around that object using the plot matrix. Then, have individuals create their own story in the same way and retell.

Story from news feature

Choose a news story with a dramatic element (refugees, kidnap, sports achievement, disaster) and demonstrate - using the plot matrix - how to create a story about it, focusing on a single character's experience. Let each student have a go.

Story from a feeling

Take a feeling and use it as a stimulus for a story. Use the plot matrix with the class and then let the students have a go. Share stories in the class and discuss what makes them work.

Story from a poem

Take a poem and demonstrate using it as a stimulus for a story. Use the plot matrix to help you. Let the students have a go and share.

Beginnings, middles and endings

Give the class a place, character and problem. Let everyone write a beginning, then pass their version on. Everyone writes a middle based on the new beginning, then passes it on. Everyone writes an ending based on the new beginning and middle. Share and review.

Story from a proverb

Take a proverb and demonstrate using it as a stimulus for a story using the plot matrix. Then let the students do their own.

Fable from a positive value

Take a positive value and use it to create a fable using the plot matrix with the class. Then let the students have a go. Share and discuss.

Fable from a character flaw

Take a character flaw and create a fable showing its dangers using the plot matrix. Let the students create their own and discuss.

Story from mime

Show the class a movement or mime sequence. Have each student imagine what is going on and use it to create a story.

Story from superpower

Choose a superpower you would like to have and create a story using the plot matrix. Demonstrate with the whole class and then let the students do their own.

Story from 'whodunnit' opening

Tell the class the beginning of a 'whodunnit' and then let them complete the story. Share some of the stories and pick a favourite. What made it work well?

Story from music

Play the class a piece of music and have them create a story inspired by the music using the plot matrix. What was it about the music that inspired the story? Was it the mood? Did it make the students think of a particular person or place?

Story from ending

Give the class an ending and have everyone write their own beginning and middle for the story. Share and review.

Story from opera clip

Show the class a clip of opera in a language they do not know. Have them discuss what might be happening. Everyone invents a story with the plot matrix based on their idea. At the end tell the class what the opera performer is singing.

Story from a movie clip

Show the class an excerpt from a movie then have them plan and create a new story inspired by the scene. Share the stories with the class.

Story from map images

Mix up images from different story maps and gets students to make a new story sequence from them. Perform the new stories to the class.

Story dice

Make story dice – one each for characters, problems, places and helpers with a different option on each face. Demonstrate with the class how to roll the dice and make up stories using each of the situations given by the dice. Let the students have a go.

Story from smell

Bring a strong-smelling item to school (coffee, perfume) - and create a story about it using the plot matrix. Have the students write their own story using a smell as inspiration.

Story from touch

Create a touch experience (hidden in a box or touch when eyes are closed) and make up a story about it with the class. Use the plot matrix to help.

Funny stories

Make up a funny story about misunderstandings. Brainstorm the misunderstandings first. Then let each student create their own.

Story from health issue

Think of a health issue - like smoking or exercise - and create a cautionary tale or inspirational story about it using the plot matrix. Let the students create and share their own.

Seven basic plots

Booker's (2004) seven basic plots are:

- Voyage and return
- Rags to riches
- Overcoming the monster
- Comedy
- Tragedy
- Quest
- Rebirth

Choose one of the seven basic plots and demonstrate making up a story using the appropriate plot matrix grid (see Annex 2). Let the students have a go. Share and review.

Story from video game

Choose a video game you know and make up a story using the characters and problems involved. Let the students have a go individually or in small groups.

One day last week

Choose one day last week and retell what happened to you as a story with clear moods and exaggerating as needed to make a good story. Let the students have a go and share with the class.

References

Booker, C (2004) **The Seven Basic Plots** Continuum International Publishing Group.

Smith, C and **Guillain, A** (2014) **The Storytelling School Handbook for Teachers,** Hawthorn Press.

Smith, C and **Guillain, A** (2014) **147 Traditional Stories for Primary School Children to Retell,** Hawthorn Press.

Smith, C and **Pottle, J** (2015) **Science Through Stories,** Hawthorn Press.

Smith, C, **Guillain, A** and **Noonan, N** (2016) **History Through Stories,** Hawthorn Press.

Glossary

Boxing for purpose: A way of planning a piece of writing by dividing it up into sections and describing the main purpose of each section.

Character quality: The core nature of a character, sometimes known as the character spine.

Creation (story creation): Making up a new story without reference to an old one.

Deepen: Expand the depth of understanding of a story cognitively, imaginatively and linguistically.

Exemplar texts: Pieces of writing to show the class as a good example of a particular writing feature.

Generate-Reflect-Select (GRS): A model for creativity, used in shared teaching and independent creativity: first generate ideas, then reflect on them before choosing one to use.

Guide texts: A text written by a teacher to prepare the questions to ask the class during a shared writing session.

Hear-Map-Step-Speak (HMSS): A way of learning a sequence orally by hearing it, mapping it, stepping it and speaking it.

Map (as in story map): A sequence of simple images which act as markers for key story moments.

Mood map: Key story moments are plotted on a graph where time is the horizontal axis and mood is on the vertical axis. Happy moods are higher and sad moods are lower with a simple image for each moment.

Multi-sensory description: Using the various senses (sight, hearing, smell, touch and taste) to evoke something in a story.

Nine story building blocks: The nine elements to consider when telling or writing a story:
- **Mood** that moves us
- **Openings** that hook
- **Settings** that convince

- **Characters** we care about
- **Problems** that matter
- **Middles** that build drama
- **Endings** that satisfy
- **Action** that is clear
- **Description** that is vivid

Plot matrix: A nine box matrix for story-making and planning.

Where?	Who?	What's the problem?
Setback 1	Setback 2	Helpers
Solution	Ending	Learning

Problem (in a story): The story 'problem' is the core difficulty which the main character faces. Story problems normally correspond to core human needs of one kind or another. For a story to work, the audience needs to care about the problem.

Recycle: Creating a new story from an old one, usually by substitution, re-using the pattern, changing the point of view or adding sequels and prequels.

Re-telling: Taking a known story and performing it in the storyteller's own words.

Seven Basic Plots: Booker's seven common story patterns:
- Voyage and return
- Rags to riches
- Overcoming the monster
- Comedy
- Tragedy
- Quest
- Rebirth

Shared writing: A way of teaching writing by creating a text using input from a class or group so they experience how to create a text.

Show-don't-tell: Evoking a feeling or quality in a character, not by naming it but by describing actions, expressions, thoughts and bodily responses.

Six ways of thinking and communicating (6TCs): These correspond to the 6 'non-fiction' forms often taught in primary school: discussion, persuasion, explanation, instruction, recount and information report.

Step (a story): This is a way of remembering a story by walking across 'stepping-stones'. Each stone is a key moment in a story and the stepper creates a gesture and phrase to help remember it.

Storytelling Schools: A method of learning using oral storytelling as the springboard for learning combining oracy, literacy and creativity.

Toolkit (as in writing toolkit): This is a summary of techniques used to achieve a certain effect.

Annex 1. Plot Matrix Planning Sheet

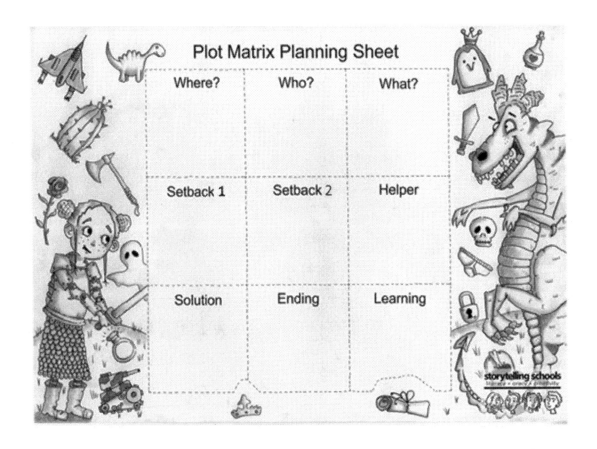

Plot Matrix Planning Sheet

Where?	Who?	What?
Setback 1	Setback 2	Helper
Solution	Ending	Learning

storytelling schools

Annex 2. The Seven Basic Plots Planning Grids

Plot	Who?	What problem?	Resolution/ Ending	Learning
Overcome Monster	Hero	Evil monster causes suffering	Monster overcome or killed	Courage Perseverance Cleverness
Rags to Riches	Poor, likeable	Oppressed, victimized, poor and unfulfilled	Emancipated, empowered, rich and happy.	Kindness Cleverness Fairness
Voyage and Return	Explorer	Survive and return from new land	Home with new qualities	Courage Understanding
Quest	Hero	Particular goal, often with reward	Goals achieved, much learned	Courage
Comedy	Fools	Misunderstandings	The moment of realisation (or not)	Understandings
Tragedy	Flawed protagonist	A calling or goal that will deliver personal pain	Unsatisfactory	Consequences of flaw
Rebirth	Anyone	Something causing unhappiness - often self-imposed	Transformed	Perspective radically changed

Annex 3. Detailed Index

Speaking and Listening Games   **6**

    Tell me more   6
    Tell me more lies   7
    Tell me more fiction   7
    Fortunately - unfortunately   7
    Why - because   7
    Why - because for fiction   8
    City of Rome   8
    Spot the lie   8
    Repetition   8

Re-telling a Story by Heart   **10**

    Tell it and map it   10
    Tell it and step it   11
    Tell it in pairs with a talking stick   12
    Tell it in a talking circle   12
    Story circle performance   12
    Tell another class a story   12
    Card sorting   12
    Learn from a storyteller clip   12
    Reflecting circle retelling   13

Story Comprehension   **16**

    Reflecting circle for story appreciation   16
    Mood map   16
    Plot matrix   17
    Character by role on the wall   19
    Character by phone   19
    Character profile   19
    Quiz   19
    Character from movie clip   20
    Ending debate   20
    Tweet re-telling   20
    Movie plot summary   20
    Basic plots   20

Drama   **22**

    Whole class re-enactment   22

Re-enactment and word-storming 22
Phone home 22
Dialogue role play 22
Hot seat 23
Job interview 23
Puppet retelling 23
Freeze-frames 23
Acting out key scenes 23
TV chat show improvisation 24
This is Your Life 24
Courtroom drama 24
Mannequin modelling 24
Toys and props 24
Tell and mime 24

Music **26**

Fitting songs to the steps 26
Creating songs to the steps 26
Instruments and soundscapes 27

Movement **29**

Reflecting circle 29
Story Stepping 29
Class dance 29
Group dance 29
Steps into Dance 29
Song into dance 30
Group dance (by genre) 30

Poetry **32**

Word pattern poem 34
Poem into song 34
Recycle a poem 34
Poem from picture 34
Narrative poem from pictures 34
Movie poem 34
Book poem 35
Poem from a name (acrostic) 35
Question poem 35
Praise poem 35
Bragging poems 35

Art, Design and Digital   **37**

    Story picture exhibition   37
    Cartoon re-telling   37
    Giant story map   37
    Shoe box setting   37
    Prop making   37
    Stop-start   38
    Lego or plasticine re-telling   38
    Green screen   38
    Record storytelling   38

Other Curriculum Links   **40**

    Research   40
    Reading   40
    Non-fiction   40
    Experiences   40
    Science   40
    Values   41
    History   41
    Geography   41
    Maths   41
    Citizenship   41
    Other languages   41
    Emotional literacy   41

Story Writing   **43**

    Mood mapping and writing   43
    Multisensory writing   43
    Wanted poster   43
    Postcards home   43
    Diary entry   43
    Monologue   44
    Thought and speech bubbles   44
    Setting   44
    Text messaging   44
    Descriptive zooming   44
    Story pitch   44
    Movie pitch   44
    Facebook / Instagram   44
    Newspaper report   45
    Play script   45

Texts   45
Emails   45
Newspaper article   45
Rewrite a song-story   45
Flashback writing   45
Mood practice   45
Setting writing   46
Suspense writing practice   46
Dilemma writing   46
Multisensory openings   46
Mono-sensory openings   46
Dialogue between first and last   46
Show-don't-tell mood practice   46
Show-don't-tell character practice   46
Dating site profile   47
Obituary   47
Object writing   47
Therapist advice   47

Story Recycling   49

Reset in a modern context   49
Find a new ending   49
Recycle with substitution   50
Recycle with plot pattern   50
Recycle with a new point of view   50
Back-stories   50

Story Creation   52

Story from character and object   53
Shared story-making from an object   53
Word story circle   53
Sentence story circle   53
Fortunately - unfortunately   53
Story from known object   53
Story from news feature   53
Story from a feeling   54
Story from a poem   54
Beginnings, middles and endings   54
Story from a proverb   54
Fable from a positive value   54
Fable from a character flaw   54
Story from mime   54

Story from superpower   54
Story from 'whodunnit' opening   55
Story from music   55
Story from ending   55
Story from opera clip   55
Story from a movie clip   55
Story from map images   55
Story dice   55
Story from smell   56
Story from touch   56
Funny stories   56
Story from health issue   56
Seven basic plots   56
Story from video game   56
One day last week   57

Annex 4. Alphabetical Index

Acting out key scenes	23
Back-stories	50
Basic plots	20
Beginnings, middles and endings	54
Book poem	35
Bragging poems	35
Card sorting	12
Cartoon re-telling	37
Character by phone	19
Character by role on the wall	19
Character from movie clip	20
Character profile	19
Citizenship	41
City of Rome	8
Class dance	29
Courtroom drama	24
Creating songs to the steps	26
Dating site profile	47
Descriptive zooming	44
Dialogue between first and last	46
Dialogue role play	22
Diary entry	43
Dilemma writing	46
Emails	45
Emotional literacy	41
Ending debate	20
Experiences	40
Fable from a character flaw	54
Fable from a positive value	54
Facebook / Instagram	44
Find a new ending	49
Fitting songs to the steps	26
Flashback writing	45
Fortunately - unfortunately	7
Fortunately - unfortunately	53
Freeze-frames	23

Funny stories	56
Geography	41
Giant story map	37
Green screen	38
Group dance	29
Group dance (by genre)	30
History	41
Hot seat	23
Instruments and soundscapes	27
Job interview	23
Learn from a storyteller clip	12
Lego or plasticine re-telling	38
Mannequin modelling	24
Maths	41
Monologue	44
Mono-sensory openings	46
Mood map	16
Mood mapping and writing	43
Mood practice	45
Movie pitch	44
Movie plot summary	20
Movie poem	34
Multisensory openings	46
Multisensory writing	43
Narrative poem from pictures	34
Newspaper article	45
Newspaper report	45
Non-fiction	40
Obituary	47
Object writing	47
One day last week	57
Other languages	41
Phone home	22
Play script	45
Plot matrix	17
Poem from a name (acrostic)	35
Poem from picture	34
Poem into song	34

Postcards home	43
Praise poem	35
Prop making	37
Puppet retelling	23
Question poem	35
Quiz	19
Reading	40
Record storytelling	38
Recycle a poem	34
Recycle with a new point of view	50
Recycle with plot pattern	50
Recycle with substitution	50
Re-enactment and word-storming	22
Reflecting circle	29
Reflecting circle for story appreciation	16
Reflecting circle retelling	13
Repetition	8
Research	40
Reset in a modern context	49
Rewrite a song-story	45
Science	40
Sentence story circle	53
Setting	44
Setting writing	46
Seven basic plots	56
Shared story-making from an object	53
Shoe box setting	37
Show-don't-tell character practice	46
Show-don't-tell mood practice	46
Song into dance	30
Spot the lie	8
Steps into Dance	29
Stop-start	38
Story circle performance	12
Story dice	55
Story from 'whodunnit' opening	55
Story from a feeling	54
Story from a movie clip	55

Story from a poem	54
Story from a proverb	54
Story from character and object	53
Story from ending	55
Story from health issue	56
Story from known object	53
Story from map images	55
Story from mime	54
Story from music	55
Story from news feature	53
Story from opera clip	55
Story from smell	56
Story from superpower	54
Story from touch	56
Story from video game	56
Story picture exhibition	37
Story pitch	44
Story Stepping	29
Suspense writing practice	46
Tell and mime	24
Tell another class a story	12
Tell it and map it	10
Tell it and step it	11
Tell it in a talking circle	12
Tell it in pairs with a talking stick	12
Tell me more	6
Tell me more fiction	7
Tell me more lies	7
Text messaging	44
Texts	45
Therapist advice	47
This is Your Life	24
Thought and speech bubbles	44
Toys and props	24
TV chat show improvisation	24
Tweet re-telling	20
Values	41
Wanted poster	43

Whole class re-enactment   22

Why - because   7

Why - because for fiction   8

Word pattern poem   34

Word story circle   53

Printed in Great Britain
by Amazon

43558034R00045